NBA BOOK OF BESTS

by John Hareas

SCHOLASTIC INC.

New York   Toronto   London   Auckland   Sydney
Mexico City   New Delhi   Hong Kong   Buenos Aires

To Jennifer, Emma and Christopher — my best of the best.

The NBA is an ultra-elite group.

To gain membership, you don't just have to be good. You have to be better than good—you have to be great. More than *3,000* players have logged at least one NBA minute in the 56-year history of the league. Only a select few have become NBA superstars. Who are they? They are the all-time leading scorers, rebounders and shotblockers. The game's greatest players. You know their names. Abdul-Jabbar. Jordan. Chamberlain. Malone (Moses and Karl). Stockton. Erving. O'Neal. Duncan. Miller. Iverson.

And there are more, of course. This book features the players whose greatness on the court has won them fans all over the world and has had a huge impact on the game itself.

Beyond the incredible stats, the *NBA Book of Bests* features plenty of other mind-boggling records. Did you know that in the history of the NBA, there have been only *eight* players who have stood 5–7 or shorter? And, on the flip side, that there have been only *eight* players who stood 7–4 or taller?

Go beyond the numbers and illustrate your very own record-breaking plays on the foldout wipe-off board that accompanies this book. Points, rebounds and assists are the result of carefully executed plays, and you can draw up your very own! Then write in your own stats as you track your favorite players throughout the season. That way, you can decide for yourself which players are the very *best of the best*!

HIGHEST SCORERS

TOP 10 NBA CAREER SCORERS
(10,000 or more points)

PLAYER	PTS	AVG
Kareem Abdul-Jabbar	38,387	24.6
Karl Malone	**34,707**	**25.7**
Wilt Chamberlain	31,419	30.1
Michael Jordan	**30,652**	**31.0**
Moses Malone	27,409	20.6
Elvin Hayes	27,313	21.0
Hakeem Olajuwon	**26,946**	**21.8**
Oscar Robertson	26,710	25.7
Dominique Wilkins	26,668	24.8
John Havlicek	26,395	20.8

FUN FACT: Kareem Abdul-Jabbar won six Most Valuable Player awards, the most in NBA history!

NBA PLAYOFFS: HIGHEST SCORERS AVERAGE
(400 Games or 10,000 Points Minimum)

PLAYER	PTS	AVG
Michael Jordan	**30,652**	**31.0**
Wilt Chamberlain	31,419	30.1
Shaquille O'Neal	**18,634**	**27.6**
Elgin Baylor	23,149	27.4
Jerry West	25,192	27.0
Allen Iverson	**10,908**	**26.9**
Bob Pettit	20,880	26.4
George Gervin	20,708	26.2
Oscar Robertson	26,710	25.7
Karl Malone	**34,707**	**25.7**

FUN FACT: Michael always wears his University of North Carolina shorts under his uniform for good luck.

NBA PLAYOFFS—MOST POINTS

NBA PLAYOFFS — MOST POINTS (Active Players)

PLAYER	PTS
Michael Jordan	5,987
Karl Malone	4,421
Hakeem Olajuwon	3,755
Scottie Pippen	3,619
Shaquille O'Neal	3,497
Patrick Ewing	2,813
Reggie Miller	2,563
John Stockton	2,380
David Robinson	2,041
Horace Grant	1,907

FUN FACT: Karl Malone holds the single-game playoff record for most free throws made in a game. He delivered an 18-for-18 performance against the Los Angeles Lakers on May 10, 1997.

* Names in **bold** indicate active players.

NBA PLAYOFFS TOP 10 NBA CAREER SCORERS (1,000 or more points)

PLAYER	PTS
Michael Jordan	**5,987**
Kareem Abdul-Jabbar	5,762
Jerry West	4,457
Karl Malone	**4,421**
Larry Bird	3,897
John Havlicek	3,776
Hakeem Olajuwon	**3,755**
Magic Johnson	3,701
Elgin Baylor	3,623
Scottie Pippen	**3,619**

FUN FACT: One of the greatest players in NBA history, Larry Bird led the Boston Celtics to three NBA titles (1981, 1984, 1986).

HIGHEST SCORING AVERAGE (Active Players)
(25 games or 625 points minimum)

PLAYER	G	FGM	FTM	PTS	AVG
Michael Jordan	179	2,188	1,463	5,987	33.4
Allen Iverson	45	481	317	1,363	30.3
Shaquille O'Neal	124	1,355	787	3,497	28.2
Karl Malone	167	1,611	1,193	4,421	26.5
Hakeem Olajuwon	145	1,504	743	3,755	25.9
Ray Allen	26	223	107	629	24.2
Tim Duncan	48	419	306	1,146	23.9
Reggie Miller	109	819	654	2,563	23.5
Anfernee Hardaway	54	406	263	1,162	21.5
Chris Webber	40	355	137	855	21.4

FUN FACT: Allen Iverson of the Philadelphia 76ers scored 40 points in five straight games in April 1997 to set an NBA rookie record.

MOST POINTS (Active Players)

PLAYER	POINTS
Michael Jordan	5,987
Karl Malone	4,421
Hakeem Olajuwon	3,755
Scottie Pippen	3,619
Shaquille O'Neal	3,497
Patrick Ewing	2,813
Reggie Miller	2,563
John Stockton	2,380
David Robinson	2,041
Horace Grant	1,907

FUN FACT: Shaquille is a two-time NBA scoring champion. He averaged 36.3 points in the Los Angeles Lakers' sweep of the New Jersey Nets in the 2002 NBA Finals.

MOST GAMES PLAYED

★ Names in **bold** indicate active players.

ALL-TIME: NBA REGULAR SEASON

PLAYER	GAMES
Robert Parish	1,611
Kareem Abdul-Jabbar	1,560
John Stockton	**1,422**
Karl Malone	**1,353**
Moses Malone	1,329
Buck Williams	1,307
Elvin Hayes	1,303
Sam Perkins	1,286
A.C. Green	1,278
Terry Porter	**1,274**

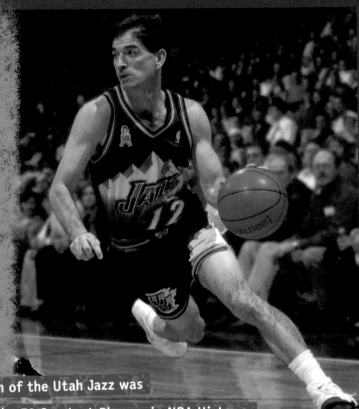

FUN FACT: In 1996, point guard John Stockton of the Utah Jazz was selected as one of the 50 Greatest Players in NBA History.

NBA PLAYOFFS (Active Players)

PLAYER	GAMES
Scottie Pippen	204
Michael Jordan	179
John Stockton	177
Horace Grant	170
Karl Malone	167
Robert Horry	153
Hakeem Olajuwon	145
Charles Oakley	144
Derrick McKey	142
Patrick Ewing	139

FUN FACT: Scottie Pippen of the Portland Trail Blazers accumulated most of his playoff experience as a valuable member of the Chicago Bulls, where he helped them win six titles in eight seasons

MOST MINUTES PLAYED

ALL-TIME: NBA REGULAR SEASON

PLAYER	MINUTES
Kareem Abdul-Jabbar	57,446
Karl Malone	**50,543**
Elvin Hayes	50,000
Wilt Chamberlain	47,859
John Havlicek	46,471
Robert Parish	45,704
John Stockton	**45,489**
Moses Malone	45,071
Hakeem Olajuwon	**44,222**
Oscar Robertson	43,886

FUN FACT: Oscar Robertson averaged a triple double during the 1961–62 season. The Big O posted an average of 30.8 points, 12.5 rebounds and 11.4 assists that season!

NBA PLAYOFFS (Active Players)

PLAYER	MINUTES
Scottie Pippen	**8,030**
Michael Jordan	**7,474**
Karl Malone	**6,918**
John Stockton	**6,249**
Horace Grant	**6,172**
Hakeem Olajuwon	**5,749**
Patrick Ewing	**5,207**
Charles Oakley	**5,108**
Shaquille O'Neal	**4,984**
Robert Horry	**4,882**

FUN FACT: Horace Grant of the Orlando Magic won three championship rings with the Chicago Bulls (1991, 1992, 1993) and one with the Los Angeles Lakers (2001).

MOST FIELD GOALS MADE

ALL-TIME NBA LEADERS

PLAYER	FGM
Kareem Abdul-Jabbar	15,837
Karl Malone	**12,740**
Wilt Chamberlain	12,681
Michael Jordan	**11,513**
Elvin Hayes	10,976
Hakeem Olajuwon	**10,749**
Alex English	10,659
John Havlicek	10,513
Dominique Wilkins	9,963
Patrick Ewing	**9,702**

FUN FACT: Hakeem Olajuwon played 17 seasons in Houston and led the Rockets to back-to-back championships. The 12-time NBA All-Star center now plays for the Toronto Raptors.

NBA PLAYOFFS (Active Players)

PLAYER	FGM
Michael Jordan	**2,188**
Karl Malone	**1,611**
Hakeem Olajuwon	**1,504**
Shaquille O'Neal	**1,355**
Scottie Pippen	**1,326**
Patrick Ewing	**1,104**
John Stockton	**837**
Reggie Miller	**819**
Horace Grant	**786**
David Robinson	**704**

FUN FACT: In 13 NBA seasons, David Robinson has played in 100 playoff games. He helped the San Antonio Spurs win the NBA championship in 1999.

MOST FIELD GOALS ATTEMPTED

ALL-TIME NBA LEADERS

PLAYER	FGA
Kareem Abdul-Jabbar	28,307
Karl Malone	**24,521**
Elvin Hayes	24,272
John Havlicek	23,930
Wilt Chamberlain	23,497
Michael Jordan	**23,010**
Dominique Wilkins	21,589
Alex English	21,036
Hakeem Olajuwon	**20,991**
Elgin Baylor	20,171

FUN FACT: Eight-time NBA All-Star Alex English, who scored 25,613 points in his career, was the first player in NBA history to score 2,000 points in eight straight seasons.

NBA PLAYOFFS (Active Players)

PLAYER	FGA
Michael Jordan	**4,497**
Karl Malone	3,466
Scottie Pippen	**2,987**
Hakeem Olajuwon	**2,847**
Shaquille O'Neal	**2,418**
Patrick Ewing	**2,353**
Reggie Miller	**1,787**
John Stockton	**1,770**
David Robinson	**1,486**
Horace Grant	**1,483**

FUN FACT: Karl Malone has participated in the playoffs in all 17 of his NBA seasons. He ranks second on the all-time list for most consecutive seasons in the NBA Playoffs, trailing his teammate John Stockton (18).

HIGHEST FIELD GOAL PERCENTAGE

★ Names in **bold** indicate active players.

ALL-TIME NBA LEADERS (2,000 FGM minimum)

PLAYER	FGM	FGA	PCT
Artis Gilmore	5,732	9,570	.599
Mark West	2,528	4,356	.580
Shaquille O'Neal	7,421	12,861	.577
Darryl Dawkins	3,477	6,079	.572
Steve Johnson	2,841	4,965	.572
James Donaldson	3,105	5,442	.571
Jeff Ruland	2,105	3,734	.564
Kareem Abdul-Jabbar	15,837	28,307	.559
Kevin McHale	6,830	12,334	.554
Bobby Jones	3,412	6,199	.550

FUN FACT: Bobby Jones of the Philadelphia 76ers was the first recipient of the NBA's Sixth Man Award. He received the honor after the 1982–83 season.

NBA PLAYOFFS (Active Players)
(150 FGM minimum)

PLAYER	FGM	FGA	PCT
Shaquille O'Neal	1,355	2,418	.560
Dale Davis	323	591	.547
Horace Grant	786	1,483	.530
Hakeem Olajuwon	1,504	2,847	.528
Anthony Mason	326	619	.527
Dikembe Mutombo	277	538	.515
Danny Manning	246	490	.502
Shawn Kemp	506	1,011	.500
Scott Williams	190	383	.496
Tim Duncan	419	849	.494

FUN FACT: Dikembe Mutombo shoots a high percentage from the field and is also a dominating defensive presence. Mutombo has won NBA Defensive Player of the Year honors a record four times.

MOST FREE THROWS MADE

ALL-TIME NBA LEADERS

PLAYER	FTM
Karl Malone	**9,145**
Moses Malone	8,531
Oscar Robertson	7,694
Jerry West	7,160
Michael Jordan	**7,061**
Dolph Schayes	6,979
Adrian Dantley	6,832
Kareem Abdul-Jabbar	6,712
Charles Barkley	6,349
Bob Pettit	6,182

FUN FACT: In 16 NBA seasons, superstar Charles Barkley made .735 percent of his free throws.

NBA PLAYOFFS (Active Players)

PLAYER	FTM
Michael Jordan	**1,463**
Karl Malone	**1,193**
Shaquille O'Neal	**787**
Scottie Pippen	**770**
Hakeem Olajuwon	**743**
Reggie Miller	**654**
David Robinson	**632**
Patrick Ewing	**597**
John Stockton	**595**
Shawn Kemp	**486**

FUN FACT: Shaquille O'Neal shot .555 percent from the free throw line last season but improved upon those numbers in the playoffs, shooting .649 on the way to the Laker's third consecutive title.

MOST FREE THROWS ATTEMPTED

ALL-TIME NBA LEADERS

PLAYER	FTA
Karl Malone	**12,342**
Wilt Chamberlain	11,862
Moses Malone	11,090
Kareem Abdul-Jabbar	9,304
Oscar Robertson	9,185
Jerry West	8,801
Charles Barkley	8,643
Michael Jordan	**8,448**
Adrian Dantley	8,351
Dolph Schayes	8,274

FUN FACT: Hall of Famer Jerry West, who played for the Los Angeles Lakers, holds the single-season record for most free throws made—840, made in the 1965–66 season.

NBA PLAYOFFS (Active Players)

PLAYER	FTA
Michael Jordan	**1,766**
Karl Malone	**1,611**
Shaquille O'Neal	**1,503**
Scottie Pippen	**1,065**
Hakeem Olajuwon	**1,034**
David Robinson	**888**
Patrick Ewing	**831**
John Stockton	**739**
Reggie Miller	**737**
Shawn Kemp	**610**

FUN FACT: In his rookie season, Karl Malone shot .481 percent from the free throw line. Now, 16 seasons later, the All-Star power forward is a career .741 percent shooter!

HIGHEST FREE THROW PERCENTAGE

* Names in **bold** indicate active players.

ALL-TIME NBA LEADERS (1,200 FTM minimum)

PLAYER	FTM	FTA	PCT
Mark Price	2,135	2,362	.904
Rick Barry	3,818	4,243	.900
Calvin Murphy	3,445	3,864	.892
Scott Skiles	1,548	1,741	.889
Larry Bird	3,960	4,471	.886
Reggie Miller	**5,634**	**6,363**	**.885**
Bill Sharman	3,143	3,559	.883
Jeff Hornacek	2,973	3,390	.877
Ray Allen	**1,638**	**1,870**	**.876**
Ricky Pierce	3,389	3,871	.875

FUN FACT: Reggie Miller of the Indiana Pacers led the NBA in free throw percentage three times. He placed second in the 2001–02 season with a .919 mark.

NBA PLAYOFFS (Active Players)
(100 FTM minimum)

PLAYER	FTM	FTA	PCT
Peja Stojakovic	104	113	.920
Reggie Miller	654	737	.887
Ray Allen	107	121	.884
Allan Houston	268	303	.884
Dirk Nowitzki	148	168	.881
Steve Smith	308	359	.858
Sam Cassell	274	322	.851
Glen Rice	169	200	.845
Michael Jordan	1,463	1,766	.828
Terry Porter	437	529	.826

FUN FACT: Peja Stojakovic excels from both the free throw line and the three-point line. The Sacramento Kings All-Star forward won the 1 800 CALL ATT Shootout at the 2002 NBA All-Star Saturday Night in Philadelphia.

MOST THREE-POINT FIELD GOALS MADE

★ Names in **bold** indicate active players.

ALL-TIME NBA LEADERS

PLAYER	3FGM
Reggie Miller	2,217
Dale Ellis	1,719
Tim Hardaway	1,531
Glen Rice	1,453
Dan Majerle	1,360
Mitch Richmond	1,326
Terry Porter	1,297
Mookie Blaylock	1,283
Vernon Maxwell	1,256
Dell Curry	1,245

FUN FACT: Dell Curry, who rains jumpers for the Toronto Raptors, played for the Hornets and is the franchise's all-time leading scorer with 9,839 points.

NBA PLAYOFFS (Active Players)

PLAYER	3FGM
Reggie Miller	271
Scottie Pippen	197
Robert Horry	189
Dan Majerle	181
John Starks	176
Terry Porter	151
Michael Jordan	148
Steve Smith	128
Bryon Russell	126
Mookie Blaylock	125

FUN FACT: Steve Smith shoots well from the three-point line but he also knows how to dish—big time. Smith donated $2.5 million to his alma mater, Michigan State, to build the Clara Bell Smith Student Activity Center, in honor of his late mother.

HIGHEST THREE-POINT FIELD GOAL PERCENTAGE

NBA ALL-TIME LEADERS
(250 3FGM Minimum)

PLAYER	3FGM	3FGA	PCT
Steve Kerr	677	1,475	.459
Hubert Davis	716	1,614	.444
Drazen Petrovic	255	583	.437
Tim Legler	260	603	.431
B.J. Armstrong	436	1,026	.425
Pat Garrity	352	835	.422
Steve Nash	458	1,092	.419
Wesley Person	954	2,296	.416
Dana Barros	1,090	2,652	.411
Trent Tucker	575	1,410	.408

FUN FACT: As a member of the Cleveland Cavaliers, Steve Kerr led the NBA with a .507 three-point field goal percentage in 1989–90. He accomplished the same feat with the Chicago Bulls in 1994–95 (.524).

NBA PLAYOFFS (35 3FGM minimum)

PLAYER	3FGM	3FGA	PCT
Ray Allen	76	164	.463
Keith Van Horn	37	86	.430
Allan Houston	76	181	.420
Eddie Jones	67	160	.419
Voshon Lenard	54	131	.412
Steve Nash	38	93	.409
Reggie Miller	271	665	.408
David Wesley	43	106	.406
Steve Smith	128	322	.398
Derek Fisher	92	232	.397

FUN FACT: One of the NBA's best three-point shooters, Ray Allen shares the single-game playoff record for most three-point field goals made in one quarter: five (May 11, 1999, at Indiana).

MOST TOTAL REBOUNDS

NBA ALL-TIME LEADERS

PLAYER	REBOUNDS
Wilt Chamberlain	23,924
Bill Russell	21,620
Kareem Abdul-Jabbar	17,440
Elvin Hayes	16,279
Moses Malone	16,212
Robert Parish	14,715
Nate Thurmond	14,464
Walt Bellamy	14,241
Karl Malone	**13,973**
Wes Unseld	13,769

FUN FACT: Wilt Chamberlain wasn't just a great rebounder. He was one of the NBA's greatest scorers. He once scored 100 points in a single game!

NBA PLAYOFFS (Active Players)

PLAYER	REBOUNDS
Karl Malone	**1,843**
Hakeem Olajuwon	**1,621**
Scottie Pippen	**1,572**
Shaquille O'Neal	**1,571**
Horace Grant	**1,457**
Charles Oakley	**1,445**
Patrick Ewing	**1,435**
Michael Jordan	**1,152**
David Robinson	**1,149**
Robert Horry	**943**

FUN FACT: Robert Horry set an NBA Playoffs record for most three-point field goals made in a game without a miss (seven) against the Utah Jazz in Game 2 of the 1997 Western Conference Semifinals.

MOST OFFENSIVE REBOUNDS

★ Names in **bold** indicate active players.

NBA ALL-TIME LEADERS

PLAYER	REBOUNDS
Moses Malone	6,731
Robert Parish	4,598
Buck Williams	4,526
Dennis Rodman	4,329
Charles Barkley	4,260
Hakeem Olajuwon	**4,034**
Kevin Willis	**3,981**
Charles Oakley	**3,887**
Otis Thorpe	3,446
Larry Smith	3,401

FUN FACT: Robert Parish, formerly of the Boston Celtics, holds the career playoff record for most offensive rebounds—571.

NBA PLAYOFFS (Active Players)

PLAYER	REBOUNDS
Shaquille O'Neal	**568**
Horace Grant	**549**
Charles Oakley	**519**
Hakeem Olajuwon	**471**
Scottie Pippen	**464**
Karl Malone	**458**
Patrick Ewing	**337**
Dale Davis	**326**
David Robinson	**322**
Shawn Kemp	**313**

FUN FACT: Dale Davis, power forward on the Portland Trail Blazers, donates tickets for every home game to the Blazers Community ticket program.

MOST DEFENSIVE REBOUNDS

★ Names in **bold** indicate active players.

NBA ALL-TIME LEADERS

PLAYER	REBOUNDS
Karl Malone	**10,585**
Robert Parish	10,117
Hakeem Olajuwon	**9,714**
Moses Malone	9,481
Kareem Abdul-Jabbar	9,394
Patrick Ewing	**8,855**
Buck Williams	8,491
Charles Barkley	8,286
Jack Sikma	8,274
Charles Oakley	**8,206**

FUN FACT: Patrick Ewing, formerly of the Orlando Magic, is a great rebounder and a terrific shotblocker. Ewing shares the single-game record for most blocked shots—eight (June 17, 1994, vs. Houston).

NBA PLAYOFFS (Active Players)

PLAYER	REBOUNDS
Karl Malone	**1,385**
Hakeem Olajuwon	**1,150**
Scottie Pippen	**1,108**
Patrick Ewing	**1,098**
Shaquille O'Neal	**1,003**
Charles Oakley	**926**
Horace Grant	**908**
Michael Jordan	**847**
David Robinson	**827**
Robert Horry	**674**

FUN FACT: Robert Horry has quite a ring collection. He owns five NBA championship rings, two from his days as a player with the Houston Rockets and three with his current team, the Los Angeles Lakers.

MOST ASSISTS

NBA ALL-TIME LEADERS

PLAYER	ASSISTS
John Stockton	**15,177**
Magic Johnson	10,141
Oscar Robertson	9,887
Mark Jackson	**9,840**
Isiah Thomas	9,061
Rod Strickland	**7,489**
Maurice Cheeks	7,392
Lenny Wilkens	7,211
Terry Porter	**7,160**
Tim Hardaway	**7,071**

FUN FACT: Maurice Cheeks is the Philadelphia 76ers all-time assists leader with 6,212 (1978–79) and all-time steals with 1,942 (1988–89). He now coaches the Portland Trail Blazers.

NBA PLAYOFFS (Active Players)

PLAYER	ASSISTS
John Stockton	**1,813**
Scottie Pippen	**1,035**
Michael Jordan	**1,022**
Mark Jackson	**883**
Terry Porter	**624**
Gary Payton	**572**
Avery Johnson	**562**
Karl Malone	**518**
Hakeem Olajuwon	**458**
Robert Horry	**434**

FUN FACT: As a member of the Spurs, Avery Johnson hit the winning shot in Game 5 of the 1999 NBA Finals that sealed San Antonio's first NBA title.

MOST STEALS

NBA ALL-TIME LEADERS

PLAYER	STEALS
John Stockton	**3,128**
Michael Jordan	**2,391**
Maurice Cheeks	2,310
Clyde Drexler	2,207
Scottie Pippen	**2,181**
Hakeem Olajuwon	**2,162**
Alvin Robertson	2,112
Mookie Blaylock	**2,075**
Gary Payton	**2,014**
Derek Harper	1,957

FUN FACT: Clyde Drexler was one of the NBA's greatest all-around players. In 15 seasons with the Portland Trail Blazers and Houston Rockets, Drexler scored 22,195 points!

NBA PLAYOFFS (Active Players)

PLAYER	STEALS
Scottie Pippen	**395**
Michael Jordan	**376**
John Stockton	**330**
Hakeem Olajuwon	**245**
Karl Malone	**226**
Robert Horry	**211**
Charles Oakley	**178**
Horace Grant	**171**
Dan Majerle	**164**
Gary Payton	**156**

FUN FACT: Three-time NBA All-Star Dan Majerle shares the record for most seasons leading the league in three-point field goals made (two).

MOST BLOCKED SHOTS

NBA ALL-TIME LEADERS

PLAYER	BLOCKED SHOTS
Hakeem Olajuwon	**3,830**
Kareem Abdul-Jabbar	3,189
Mark Eaton	3,064
Patrick Ewing	**2,894**
David Robinson	**2,843**
Dikembe Mutombo	**2,836**
Tree Rollins	2,542
Robert Parish	2,361
Manute Bol	2,086
George T. Johnson	2,082

FUN FACT: Former Utah Jazz center Mark Eaton knew how to keep opponents from approaching the basket. The 7-4 center once averaged 5.56 blocks per game during the 1984–85 season!

NBA PLAYOFFS (Active Players)

PLAYER	BLOCKED SHOTS
Hakeem Olajuwon	472
Patrick Ewing	303
David Robinson	281
Shaquille O'Neal	279
Dikembe Mutombo	215
Scottie Pippen	185
Horace Grant	173
Michael Jordan	158
Alonzo Mourning	155
Greg Ostertag	154

FUN FACT: An intimidating defensive force, Alonzo Mourning twice led the NBA in blocked shots per game. He blocked an average of 3.91 shots per game in the 1998–99 season and 3.7 shots per game in the 2000–01 season.

ALL-STAR GAME BESTS

HIGHEST SCORING AVERAGE
(3 Games or 60 Pts minimum)

PLAYER	G	PTS	AVG
Kobe Bryant	**4**	**83**	**20.8**
Oscar Robertson	12	246	20.5
Bob Pettit	11	224	20.4
Michael Jordan	**12**	**242**	**20.2**
Julius Erving	11	221	20.1
Elgin Baylor	11	218	19.8
George Mikan	4	78	19.5
Paul Westphal	5	97	19.4
Tom Chambers	4	77	19.3
David Thompson	4	75	18.8

FUN FACT: At 23 years of age, Kobe Bryant of the Los Angeles Lakers became the youngest player in NBA history to win three NBA titles.

MOST ALL-STAR GAMES PLAYED

PLAYER	GAMES
Kareem Abdul-Jabbar	18
Wilt Chamberlain	13
Bob Cousy	13
John Havlicek	13
Elvin Hayes	12
Michael Jordan	**12**
Karl Malone	**12**
Hakeem Olajuwon	**12**
Oscar Robertson	12
Bill Russell	12

FUN FACT: Hall of Famer John Havlicek is the Boston Celtics all-time leading scorer with 26,395 points.

ALL-STAR GAME BESTS

MOST REBOUNDS

PLAYER	REBOUNDS
Wilt Chamberlain	197
Bob Pettit	178
Kareem Abdul-Jabbar	149
Bill Russell	139
Moses Malone	108
Dolph Schayes	105
Elgin Baylor	99
Hakeem Olajuwon	**94**
Elvin Hayes	92
Dave Cowens	81

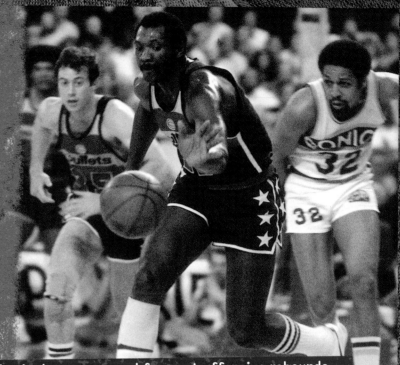

FUN FACT: Elvin Hayes shares the NBA Finals single-game record for most offensive rebounds— 11 (May 27, 1979, vs. Seattle). He played for the Washington Bullets at the time.

MOST ASSISTS

PLAYER	ASSISTS
Magic Johnson	127
Isiah Thomas	97
Bob Cousy	86
Oscar Robertson	81
Gary Payton	**71**
John Stockton	**71**
Jerry West	55
Michael Jordan	**52**
Kareem Abdul-Jabbar	51
Larry Bird	41

FUN FACT: A great all-around player, Gary Payton's single-game career high for assists is 17.

MOST WINNING COACHES

ALL-TIME
(Coaches who have won 400+ games in NBA history)

COACH	W	L	PCT
Lenny Wilkens	1,268	1,056	.546
Pat Riley	1,085	512	.679
Don Nelson	1,036	806	.562
Bill Fitch	944	1,106	.460
Red Auerbach	938	479	.662
Dick Motta	935	1,017	.479
Jack Ramsay	864	783	.525
Cotton Fitzsimmons	832	775	.518
Larry Brown	831	651	.561
Jerry Sloan	828	486	.630
Gene Shue	784	861	.477
Phil Jackson	726	258	.738
John MacLeod	707	657	.518
Red Holzman	696	604	.535
George Karl	666	459	.592
Chuck Daly	638	437	.593
Doug Moe	628	529	.543
Mike Fratello	572	465	.552
Alvin Attles	557	518	.518
Del Harris	556	457	.549
Rick Adelman	544	361	.601
K.C. Jones	522	252	.674
Kevin Loughery	474	662	.417
Alex Hannum	471	412	.533
Rudy Tomjanovich	460	358	.562
Billy Cunningham	454	196	.698
Larry Costello	430	300	.589
Tom Heinsohn	427	263	.619
John Kundla	423	302	.583

FUN FACT: Pat Riley is the only coach in NBA history to win at least 60 games in a season with three different teams and capture Coach of the Year honors with three different teams (1989–90 Los Angeles Lakers; 1992–93 New York Knicks; 1996–97 Miami Heat).

FUN FACT: Red Auerbach (pictured), legendary former coach of the Boston Celtics, and Phil Jackson, coach of the Los Angeles Lakers, each own nine NBA titles, the most in NBA history!

MOST WINNING COACHES

NBA PLAYOFFS

COACH	W	L	PCT
Phil Jackson	156	54	.743
Pat Riley	155	100	.608
Red Auerbach	99	69	.589
K.C. Jones	81	57	.587
Lenny Wilkens	80	94	.460
Jerry Sloan	77	76	.503
Chuck Daly	75	51	.595
Billy Cunningham	66	39	.629
Larry Brown	63	66	.488
John Kundla	60	35	.632
Don Nelson	59	71	.454
Red Holzman	58	47	.552
George Karl	57	63	.475
Dick Motta	56	70	.444
Bill Fitch	55	54	.505
Rick Adelman	53	50	.515
Rudy Tomjanovich	51	39	.567
Tom Heinsohn	47	33	.588
John MacLeod	47	54	.465
Alex Hannum	45	34	.570
Jack Ramsay	44	58	.431
Del Harris	38	50	.432
Larry Costello	37	23	.617
Jeff Van Gundy	37	32	.536
Cotton Fitzsimmons	35	49	.417
Bill Sharman	35	27	.565
Bill Russell	34	27	.557
Al Cervi	33	26	.559
Doug Moe	33	50	.398
Fred Schaus	33	38	.465

FUN FACT: Lenny Wilkens, who coaches the Toronto Raptors and was a former All-Star guard, most notably with the St. Louis Hawks, is enshrined in the Basketball Hall of Fame as both a player and a coach!

FUN FACT: Longtime Utah Jazz head coach Jerry Sloan played 11 seasons in the NBA, 10 of them in Chicago. The two-time All-Star is the first player to have his uniform number (4) retired by the Bulls.

MOST CHAMPIONSHIPS

MOST NBA CHAMPIONSHIPS

TEAM	CHAMPIONSHIPS
Boston Celtics	16
Los Angeles Lakers	14
Chicago Bulls	6

FUN FACT: The Boston Celtics won an incredible eight NBA championships in a row (1959–66). They won 11 championships in 13 seasons!

MOST NBA FINALS MVP HONORS

PLAYER	# OF TIMES NAMED FINALS MVP
Michael Jordan	6
Magic Johnson	3
Shaquille O'Neal	3
Kareem Abdul-Jabbar	2
Larry Bird	2
Hakeem Olajuwon	2
Willis Reed	2

FUN FACT: Willis Reed (pictured) and Michael Jordan are the only players in NBA history to win regular season MVP, All-Star MVP and Finals MVP in the same season.

BEST OVERALL RECORDS

NBA PLAYOFFS

TEAM	W	L	PCT
Los Angeles Lakers	2,621	1,616	.619
Chicago Stags*	145	92	.612
Boston Celtics	2,612	1,735	.601
Washington Capitols*	157	114	.579
Anderson Packers*	37	27	.578
San Antonio Spurs	1,196	904	.570
Phoenix Suns	1,509	1,247	.548
Portland Trail Blazers	1,417	1,175	.547
Milwaukee Bucks	1,503	1,253	.545
Utah Jazz	1,232	1,032	.544
Philadelphia 76ers	2,264	1,908	.543
Seattle SuperSonics	1,530	1,308	.539
Chicago Bulls	1,513	1,406	.518
St. Louis Bombers*	122	115	.515
New York Knickerbockers	2,234	2,109	.514
Orlando Magic	525	509	.508
Atlanta Hawks	2,107	2,067	.505
Cleveland Rebels*	30	30	.500
Houston Rockets	1,404	1,434	.495
Indianapolis Olympians*	132	137	.491
Charlotte Hornets	542	574	.486
Indiana Pacers	1,006	1,094	.479
Detroit Pistons	2,027	2,209	.479
Miami Heat	534	582	.478
Sacramento Kings	1,979	2,258	.467
Golden State Warriors	2,005	2,337	.462
Denver Nuggets	964	1,136	.459
Washington Wizards	1,523	1,796	.459
Cleveland Cavaliers	1,155	1,437	.446
Dallas Mavericks	754	1,018	.426
Toronto Raptors	224	318	.413
New Jersey Nets	854	1,246	.407
Minnesota Timberwolves	409	625	.396
Toronto Huskies*	22	38	.367
Los Angeles Clippers	925	1,667	.357
Sheboygan Redskins*	22	40	.355
Baltimore Bullets*	158	292	.351
Detroit Falcons*	20	40	.333
Waterloo Hawks*	19	43	.306
Indianapolis Jets*	18	42	.300
Providence Steamrollers*	46	122	.274
Pittsburgh Ironmen*	15	45	.250
Memphis Grizzlies	124	418	.229
Denver Nuggets*	11	51	.177

* Defunct franchise

FUN FACT: The Los Angeles Lakers franchise actually began in Minneapolis in 1948. The team moved to L.A. in 1960.

ALL-TIME TALLEST AND SHORTEST PLAYERS

TALLEST

HEIGHT	PLAYER	CAREER
7 feet, 7 inches (2.31 meters)	Manute Bol	1986–94
	Gheorghe Muresan	1994–97, Present
7 feet, 6 inches (2.28 meters)	Shawn Bradley	1994–Present
7 feet, 5 inches (2.26 meters)	Chuck Nevitt	1983–94
	Yao Ming	2002–Present
7 feet, 4 inches (2.23 meters)	Mark Eaton	1983–93
	Ralph Sampson	1984–92
	Rik Smits	1989–Present

FUN FACT: Former NBA center Gheorghe Muresan starred on the big screen! In 1998, he acted opposite Billy Crystal in the comedy *My Giant*.

SHORTEST

HEIGHT	PLAYER	CAREER
5 feet, 3 inches (1.60 meters)	Tyrone "Muggsy" Bogues	1988–Present
5 feet, 5 inches (1.65 meters)	Earl Boykins	1999–Present
5 feet, 7 inches (1.70 meters)	Greg Grant	1990–93
	Keith "Mr." Jennings	1993–95
	Red Klotz	1947–48
	Wat Misaka	1947–48
	Monte Towe	1976–77
	Anthony "Spud" Webb	1986, 1996, 1998
5 feet, 8 inches (1.73 meters)	Charlie Criss	1978–85
	Melvin Hirsch	1946–47

FUN FACT: At 5-7, Spud Webb towered over the competition when he won the NBA Slam Dunk title in Dallas in 1986.

BEST SLAM DUNKERS

CHAMPIONS

YEAR	PLAYER, TEAM
1984	Larry Nance, Phoenix Suns
1985	Dominique Wilkins, Atlanta Hawks
1986	Spud Webb, Atlanta Hawks
1987	Michael Jordan, Chicago Bulls
1988	Michael Jordan, Chicago Bulls
1989	Kenny Walker, New York Knicks
1990	Dominique Wilkins, Atlanta Hawks
1991	Dee Brown, Boston Celtics
1992	Cedric Ceballos, Phoenix Suns
1993	Harold Miner, Miami Heat
1994	Isaiah Rider, Minnesota Timberwolves
1995	Harold Miner, Miami Heat
1996	Brent Barry, Los Angeles Clippers
1997	Kobe Bryant, Los Angeles Lakers
1998	No competition held
1999	No competetion held
2000	Vince Carter, Toronto Raptors
2001	Desmond Mason, Seattle SuperSonics
2002	Jason Richardson, Golden State Warriors

FUN FACT: Kenny Walker holds the record for the highest score of any round in slam dunk contest history. He scored 148.1 in the 1989 finals, which barely bests Michael Jordan's mark of 148 in the 1987 semifinals!

ALL-TIME NBA BROTHERS

ALL-TIME LIST OF BROTHERS TO PLAY ON THE SAME TEAM

BROTHERS	SEASONS	TEAM
Tom & Dick Van Arsdale	1976–77	Phoenix Suns
Caldwell & Charles Jones	1984–85	Chicago Bulls
Caldwell & Major Jones	1982–84	Houston Rockets
Al & Dick McGuire	1951–54	New York Knicks
Don & Mac Otten	1949–50	Tri-Cities Blackhawks
George & Henry Pearcy	1946–47	Detroit Falcons
Mark & Brent Price	1995–96	Washington Bullets
Connie & John Simmons	1946–47	Boston Celtics
Dominique & Gerald Wilkins	1998–99	Orlando Magic

FUN FACT: Dominique (pictured) and Gerald Wilkins are the highest scoring brother duo in NBA history, with a combined 38,404 points. Both brothers also played a combined 28 seasons in the NBA.

ALL-TIME NBA COACHING BROTHERS

BROTHERS	COACH/CAREER
Herb and Larry Brown	Herb Brown/Detroit 1975–78
	Larry Brown/Carolina (ABA): 1972–74; Denver (ABA): 1974–76; Denver: 1976–79; New Jersey: 1981–83; San Antonio 1988–92; Los Angeles Clippers: 1992–93; Indiana: 1993–97; Philadelphia: 1997–Present

FUN FACT: Larry Brown, head coach of the Philadelphia 76ers, was recognized for his successful coaching career when he was enshrined in the Basketball Hall of Fame in Springfield, Massachusetts, in the fall of 2002.

ALL-TIME NBA/ABA FATHER-SON COMBOS

FATHERS	SONS
Rick Barry	Brent Barry, Drew Barry & Jon Barry
Henry Bibby	Mike Bibby
Joe "Jellybean" Bryant	Kobe Bryant
Wayne Chapman (ABA)	Rex Chapman
Rich Dumas (ABA)	Richard Dumas
Leroy Ellis	Leron Ellis
Bob Ferry	Danny Ferry
Matt Guokas, Sr.	Matt Guokas, Jr.
Earle Higgins (ABA)	Sean Higgins
Bill Hosket (NBL)	Bill Hosket
Wali Jones	Askia Jones
Ed Manning	Danny Manning
Press Maravich	Pete Maravich
Al McGuire	Allie McGuire
George Mikan	Larry Mikan
Pete Mount (NBL)	Rick Mount (ABA)
Jim Paxson, Sr.	John Paxson & Jim Paxson, Jr.
Walt Piatkowski (ABA)	Eric Piatkowski
Jimmy Walker	Jalen Rose
Dolph Schayes	Danny Schayes
Bill "Butch" Van Breda Kolff	Jan Van Breda Kolff
Ernie Vandeweghe	Kiki Vandeweghe
David Vaughn (ABA)	David Vaughn

FUN FACT: In one of the greatest upsets in NBA Finals history, the Golden State Warriors, led by Rick Barry, swept the heavily favored Washington Bullets.